POP CORPSE

Lara Glenum

ACTIONBOOKS

Notre Dame, Indiana 2013

Action Books
Joyelle McSweeney and Johannes Göransson, *Editors*
Lynda Letona and Megan Elise, 2012-13 *Editorial Assistants*

Action Books
356 O'Shaughnessy Hall
Notre Dame, IN 46556
www.actionbooks.org

First Edition

Library of Congress Control Number: 2013931619
ISBN 978-0-9831480-5-0

BOOK AND COVER DESIGN by Andrew Shuta

POP CORPSE

by Lara Glenum

"I know what you want, Princess," trilled the Sea Witch. "You want to ditch your fish tail & grow two flesh supports instead—like humans on land!—so the Prince will fall in love with you." & Then the witch laughed so loud & disgustingly that toads & snakes fell to the ground, wriggling about. "Your tail will disappear & shrink up into what humans call 'legs.' Every step you take will feel as though you're treading on knives, as though blood will flow. Now stick out your little tongue so I can cut it out as my payment."

—Hans Christian Andersen, "The Little Mermaid"

[THIS POEM IS MY VOCAL PROSTHESIS]

SCENE: There is no land. Only floating islands of plastic garbage.

My suffering has become frivolous & ornamental

which is to say
        it now participates in "luxury, mourning, war, cults,
        the construction of sumptuary monuments, games,
        spectacles, arts"

U are hereby invited to wars of attrition
& other showstoppers

2 spectacles of   ornament & excrement
in undersea palaces

festooned with horny mermaids

I am trying to speak in a different register
The register of candied decay

The filthy register of the halfbreed
which is
my own

I am poorly made, willful, death-leaning

I exhibit
a failure to thrive

Ill-gendered & millenarian
my flesh accrues
& decomposes

I can die & die & die

Club Me [Opening Score]

The seal flesh   bezerking in my pants
says no + yes

My glass eye rolls   across the wooden sea

The ha ha albino sky
rotting like meat in my throat

Sink yr seabunny fingers
in2 my creamo dreamo seal meat

Ensorcel yrself
4-evah
in loaves of hottie blubber

Well a mermaid is made of seal meat

A mermaid with a chopped-off tail
is all holes
open 2   whatevs loops thru the red tubes

The clouds are the colon of forgetting
The mermaid is the forgetting of the colon +
piss tube + snatch

O mighty fuckable   I'm cutting off my own fishtail

Plug up my wild valves
w yr skeet lotion

W yr shiny metal fingers

HERE COMES SOME MARVELOUS DEFORMATION CRAWLING TOWARD YOU IN A HUMAN SUIT!

A mermaid is supposed 2 b all seafoam

PNEUMATIC TITS! + OPALINE HAIR!

posed in ROCOCO Technicolor CORAL REEFS!!
w/spritely SEA CUCUMBERS!!   & sweet pink JELLIES!!

♥ A CUNTLESS DUMPLING!! ♥

I m so hungry for cock
I m nothing but cunt

∿∿ ∿∿ Goo-Goo Lagoon ∿∿ ∿∿

[A single spotlight on XXX, lying on a divan in a rococo undersea salon full of

kitschy trinkets. Her appearance, everything about the scene, should appear excessive & slightly off. The emphasis is on artifice & the unnatural. XXX looks bored + distracted. Her room is full of baroque oceanic taxidermy. She is fidgeting with some kind of small vessel or ornament.]

XXX:
My father is a gillygobber &
the King of the Sea

In his freakopolis the liquid children
do not go in for cuzzly wuzzly mooncalves

but I sure as fuck do

This is disgusto neophilia
say
The Daughters of Err

You are better off in limbo
than with The Smear's

sonic death monkey

These are noise-turds
says the Sea Witch

texting me
a torture memo

YR COCK BELONGS UP THE ASS OF THIS BOOK

The Smear lives on Western Garbage Flotilla 5
(aka The Isle of Noise)

He is crazy beautiful

They say he is also just plain crazy

The Smear hangs out at the undersea Yumfactory
all wowsa   in his fly threads of skullmeat

Once I saw him on a dock tying bloody fetal hares
to his torso   A lobster cage over his head

a tail light blinking in his ass cheeks

Ψ

They say when he jerks off
stars explode

& that he is opposed   to absolutely everything

Ψ After his Emergency Transport Vehicle sank
I retrieved him from the killsite

& we got deep in the freak bucket
& totes brillz
with the boo cream   his squeal cheese
whanging in my blood tanks   His human meat   Ψ

flouncing in my inexplicable hand   My cumpacked corpuscles
discharging into history   My seal meat bezerking

& Later he didn't even recognize me

                 & Still he continued riding the ETVs
           down to the Yumfactory

& I didn't approach him
cuz I got no holes to fuck with

 No legs
Nothing between

LITTLE MERDE-MAID & HER SHITSTAIN OF A STORY

(bew hew)

∿∿ The Yumfactory ∿∿

[The gilded, crenellated spires of the Yumfactory rise high above the sea floor. A pulsing, enormous wreck of a structure inlaid with gaudy gems, as though a gigantic infant ate Barbie Dream Wonderland & shat it out & rolled the turd in glittering crustaceans.

From a thousand docks, Emergency Transport Vehicles come & go, ferrying curious Land-dwellers to the Yumfactory, where

undersea denizens run illegal bazaars & obscene game parlors
& species illicitly mix.]

LAND-DWELLER *[watching the Daughters of Err enter the Yumfactory]*:
Could those bitches be any hotter?

UNDERSEA DENIZEN: Please, Air-Breather, those ain't women. They got
no holes. Not even a single shithole. They have to take shits out of their
mouths. And believe me, they take atomic dumps.

LAND-DWELLER: WTF? That's hardcore!

UNDERSEA DENIZEN: Try kissing one sometime. It's like giving a rim job to a dysentery victim. With really long ass hair.

LAND-DWELLER: Krikey! What are they?

UNDERSEA DENIZEN: Vision machines.

LAND-DWELLER: Explain?

UNDERSEA DENIZEN: Their gender was chosen for them by their parents. The King and Queen of the Sea. Who have the most to gain by keeping the current power structures in place. And they succeed not by openly oppressing us but by persistently courting/curtailing our lines of sight with the spectacle of their Vision Machines.

LAND-DWELLER: Vision Machines?

UNDERSEA DENIZEN: A culturally-produced spectacle that naturalizes highly specific forms of desire and consumption. The abject recuperated in the service of reproductive capitalism.

LAND-DWELLER *[high-pitched giggling]*: GIRLS, GIRLS, GIRLS!

[Lying on the steps of the Yumfactory, the Daughters of Err lazily begin spraying glitter all over their breasts, which are clearly fake.]

XXX:
When I first saw The Smear   I dreamt of
rinsing his pale organs
in my facehole

& fucking his eyebladders with my seafingers

& then
        selling his parts off
to the Orphaned Nihilist Society

BLUBBER SOCKET: Hawt! Tell us more, freak. *[She yawns.]*

CINDERSKELLA: Someone shut that horndog up! *[XXX laughs.]*

KINDERWHORE: Ever since the ocean's gone toxic and the earth's been burned to a crisp, she's been totes sketch.

BLUBBER SOCKET: So d'you bang The Smear yet?

XXX: Whatevs. You know I can't.

BLUBBER SOCKET *[dripping with sarcasm]*: O riiiight! Us mermaids got no sweet little glughole. All tits and noooo snatch! Poor li'l fish girls. No pleasure! All cold.

PURSED & PUCKERED: You could've used a prosthetic snatch, like everybody else, skankivore.

CINDERSKELLA: The Smear? Fo realz? Great. You've got a retard-on for a monster. Good job.

KINDERWHORE: I heard that hag-born cretin tried to rape his step-sister.

CINDERSKELLA: No, that was his dad, the Sorcerer. That huckster who told everyone he could reverse the Disaster if all the human women would just send him their used panties. Anyway. They all died in the Disaster. And now The Smear's got the Isle of Noise to himself.

BLUBBER SOCKET: I hear his Bone Palace is massive & totes baller. Throws killa raves.

CINDERSKELLA: Anyway, he prob doesn't even have a real cock. An awful lot of human cocks shriveled and fell off after the Disaster. At least half of them are probably fake.

BLUBBER SOCKET: Ooo! I want me a fake cock, too! I know some boys who'd like me to plant a hot stem in their wanghole.

PURSED & PUCKERED: You can borrow mine!

KINDERWHORE: And the awesome thing? Nobody freaking cares that it's all fake!

XXX: Well, I do, Crustylips.

KINDERWHORE: C'mon! The Disaster's like totally the best thing that's ever happened to merfolk!

XXX: The Disaster's being serially cut off from our own pleasure.

PURSED & PUCKERED: O plz. Our reversible bodies are proof that there are a thousand modes of pleasure.

XXX: Holla. Tho we're not actually reversible. We have no sex. Our bodies are a blank slate.

CINDERSKELLA: We're costumable! Consumable! Hot twinkle teens! We put the "crème" in "crème de la crème!"

BLUBBER SOCKET: Yeah, both of them!

CINDERSKELLA: And we're poly-gendered! What could be better?

XXX: We've got no sex organs. What could be worse.

KINDERWHORE: I've heard of a group of merfolk off the coast of East Garbage Flotilla 9 that can change sex at will. Like they have real, operable junk. And they can switch it around whenever they want.

XXX: Now that's a reversible body!

CINDERSKELLA: O plz. What's the diff? We're whatever anyone wants us to be. And that's hawt. No other species can claim that.

XXX: But I want my own sex.

BLUBBER SOCKET: Somebody nail that girl's fins to the floor.

PURSED & PUCKERED: But we're outrageously mod! We spiritualize consumption! We're nothing but surface!

CINDERSKELLA: Who needs interiority and agency, Sparklepants? You've always been sooo retro.

BLUBBER SOCKET: Yeah, interiority is for losers. REAL GIRLS don't need interiority. Their wham-bam pageantry is their weakness is their weapon.

XXX: Real? Lolz! Now that IS a retro term! It's like we're already in some fantastical, Technicolor afterlife, where there's nothing left but drag. We're post-gender, and that's awesome. But we can't fuck. And that sucks seahorse butt. BTW, you use the word "girl" like it's an exclusive club.

BLUBBER SOCKET: Not everyone gets to be a "girl."

CINDERSKELLA: Yeah, bitches! We're the gate-keepers to the penal colony!

XXX: I think I've somehow wound up *in* the penal colony.

CINDERSKELLA: Baby, don't let The Smear get you down. Put on your wig and fake tits! Let's go out! You'll feel so much better.

PURSED & PUCKERED: Fergit this shizzle! Let's bounce!

KINDERWHORE: Blah blah, bitches! To the Royal Disorder Panic Party!

XXX: Krikey! Mom and Dad's annual gala! I nearly forgot!

〰〰 The Royal Disorder Panic Party 〰〰

[Inside the Royal bedchambers.]

QUEEN OF THE SEA: Snap on your prosthetic cooch & get down to the Royal Disorder Panic Party this minute! Your sisters are already downstairs!

XXX: In a sec! Shut the freaking door!

XXX: Krikey   I have to go muck about among sea mutants

When what I really want   is to poke the sun out
& squirt
        myself black & blue

[Turns on webcam. Opens her cutting box & takes out scalpel. Carefully cuts a hole into her scales where her snatch should be. Lubes her finger with her spit & inserts it.]

[The Queen returns & sees XXX, looking dreamy & fingering her new hole.]

QUEEN OF THE SEA *[shrieking]*: She's cutting herself again! *[King enters. Queen sobs.]*

KING OF THE SEA: Darling, no! *[Shouts.]* Someone get her cleaned up! Shut that webcam off! You're going straight back to the Slice Ward, young lady. As soon as the Royal Panic Party is over.

XXX *[muttering]*: For fuck's sake. *[Licks blood from finger.]* Hi, Mom. Hi, Dad.

KINDERWHORE *[listening at the door]*: Geez. I don't see why it's such a problem. At least she's made a name for herself.

PURSED & PUCKERED: A name for herself? Ha! Read the headlines! She's a self-mutilating freak!

SEA PRINCESS INDULGES IN SELF-ABUSE!!

[A massive marine grotto, pulsing sick with raucous sea junk. Everything flashes & throbs. The Daughters of Err enter sporting glow-in-the-dark prosthetic snatches—all except XXX, who wears a hot pink merkin.]

MASTER OF CEREMONIES: The Royal Disorder Panic Party is getting underway! Send in the hooligan sea kittens with deracinated faces! Send in the junk bunnies with malignancy twitching in their crank holes! Send in the contammo sea ghouls! Let the festivities begin!

KINDERWHORE *[sidling up]*: How's the par-tay, grrrls?

XXX: Krikey. The usual squid.

CINDERSKELLA: It's a serious crock of bones in here tonight. There's a high level of miracle prevention.

BLUBBET SOCKET: Ooo, grrl! It's Octocock!

KINDERWHORE: $$$$$$$

XXX: Blarg.

CINDERSKELLA: And look who's right behind him!

[The Smear enters wearing cop glasses & a sequined ball-gown smeared with goat shit. The gown has a plastic window cut out for his genitals, which are painted red. He is regal & beautiful.]

XXX:
The Smear   O!

My jumble of flesh
inches up   onto the lip of this revolutionary night

[CINDERSKELLA drags XXX over to the group of bi-valve hotties The Smear has joined.]

CINDERSKELLA: Hi. You two know each other, I think?

THE SMEAR: I used to be stereotyped for my ambulance good looks and a smile that says "I just stabbed myself with the sharp end of a compass."

XXX: Um, hi.

THE SMEAR: I used to tame dead horses and count cockroaches on the gnarled arms of the downtown pretenders.

CINDERSKELLA: Downtown pretenders?

THE SMEAR: Then came the angel. It woke me up one night poking me with a rifle to check if I was asleep or imitating its dead cousin.

CINDERSKELLA: Are you on eel crack, or what?

THE SMEAR: I was imitating its dead cousin.

CINDERSKELLA *[rolling her eyes]*: Whatevs, creep. I'm gonna go swill some conch piss.

THE SMEAR: I was powerful as only a spoiled child can be. The angel was spoiled as only meat can be. It taught me to rifle through the faces of faceless victims.

OCTOCOCK *[sizing up XXX]*: You're the infamous Princess X-acto? The princess with the webcam and the cutting box, right?

BLUBBER SOCKET: Yep. She's the famous cutter alright.

XXX: It's performance art.

PURSED & PUCKERED: More like torture porn.

XXX *[blushing & turning to The Smear]*: I think we met once before? That time your ETV sank? I, um, rescued you?

THE SMEAR: It was the Year of the Scab and there was no room for people who act like lawn fires when they should be modeling the latest symptoms in remodeled scriptoriums.

PURSED & PUCKERED *[hisses at XXX]*: What's wrong with you? That guy's, like, a total freak!

BLUBBER SOCKET: I'm out. I've gotta go do my number in the floor show. *[To XXX.]* Txt me when his head explodes. BTW? You're on right after me.

XXX *[grinning]*: Ok. I gotta go.

THE SMEAR *[calling after her]*: Meet me tonight at the taxidermy museum of your choice!

BLUBBER SOCKET: Is he always like that?

OCTOCOCK: Only when he's rumored to have been alone for five weeks straight, watching seal porn and smoking his own burnt cum.

THE SMEAR *[muttering]*: I want to learn to touch you like extinct animals. So far, I've only got the panting right.

XXX *[aside]:*
In your silver aviator glasses you look like a sadist
but you are what

Look at the fantastic hole in your torso
The historical light of misery flooding through

AN EMBARASSMENT OF BITCHE$$$
(a floor show 4 FISHONISTAS)

#I m sea fairy

& U r a rude
mechanical

#Yr anus heart
gives me

a retard-on

#We've nothing
but runny bottom lotion

Let's drilll

#U fisted my future

with yr
Golly golly

Imma wreck
u   Imma fierce dumbwort

stewed in glittery monkey jizz

#U r so careless & rotten
with that cock I love
filth too

#Welcome to the IDIOTEQUE

#A girl is a spectacle is a pot of
licky holes
ripe 4 yr buttery reaming

#Shave off my mouth like a bunion
Make me   a hairless wunder Sir

Hide the hole alpha b

while I queen off to 2 vermin
humping in a wig

I am needybats

Bozo I need u
My clit lolling out

Muckling & hardfelt

Pop my dumpling plz

#Queen of dumdums

& holy warwhistles
I am eating out my own chest

in silent jubilation

No one smiles
this much blood

#I m a Teen Witch

#Oops I dropped my eyes
inside yr boi panties

& got a retard-on

#lolz

#I m a Teen Witch

#Our shell(ed) bodies
record a history of the final wars

#Put yr boss hog on my boss gloss
& crush me
w yr phenomenal junk

#Eyetwinkle hawt

U have retarded my dayz
in2 a narcoleptic stammer

A labial hiccup

#I can't find my bloody panties
+ The boneworld is ending

in explosive fright
& loud streamers

#Slutever

#Hi
I just met u

& here we r
2 hawt twinks

fucking on a benthic
brain fart

〰〰 The Royal Chambers 〰〰

KINDERWHORE: Why does she have to go back to the Slice Ward? Can't she stay if she promises to stop?

CINDERSKELLA: Don't be a crack tart! She's sicko. She needs freaking help.

KING OF THE SEA: Out! All of you! *[To XXX]* Pack your things. Now.

[XXX packs hastily, throwing her junk into a scallop-shaped suitcase.]

QUEEN OF THE SEA: Dammit, child, no sea-punk wigs! Or vibrating clams! No explosives, either!

XXX [muttering under her breath]:
During the night raids
I can do anything

like run with the firebrats & ignore you

or build funerary monuments out of my teeth

It is all so
festively boring

THE SLICE WARD
(((((((((Rehab Diary)))))))))

I bury my beautiful face in gruesome's lightning
I alakazam

in the Slice Ward   In the shellworks
I cut my filthy aquamarine kablam

The stringy tendons stringle out
A fan of eyeless worms

inlaid with precious blood clots
slopping out

In the Slice Ward
they have an electrical shower

for girls who feel 2 much Who feel
nothing
They call it
The Gate of Heaven

Girls should not be 2 visible
need 2 b Xed out

We stage our own extravagant deaths

& squirt all over
the camera

<Post to feed>

 This diary is a museum of my body

MUSEUMS R 4 THE CURATION OF DISEASE

I have a propensity for
Self-harm

Self-harmalade
spread like jelly out of open wrists

I let him reconfigure my joints
in a spray of cum

                              I could not b disarranged enuf
My newly-carved colon bursting in2 sharp stars

I could never be dead enuf
Could not manage dead

SEXY DEAD GIRLS RULE

w/pornbots & moaning automata
Boys r wicked self-cutters 2

LIVE GIRLS LIVE GIRLS LIVE GIRLS

When u r a GIRL
yr body is a CRIME LAB

They PHOTOGRAPH u at every point

Who performs the autopsy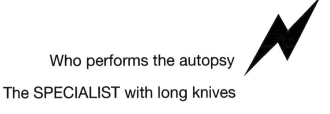

The SPECIALIST with long knives

EVERY GIRL IS SPECIAL(IST)!

The webcam is a REAL EYE

that wants 2 see me cut myself open
That wants 2 deep fuck my mouth

While I dry hump a nautilus

While I try 2 grow more nerves

[I have one shrunken fin & a discolored foretooth

                    Some of my gills are sealed shut
        along the left side]

                    DEAD GIRLS
                    DEAD GIRLS
                    DEAD GIRLS

When u finally walk in2
The Gate of Heaven

electricity will stream off
yr starparts

Scar tissue clumping under yr skin
like coal seams

Someone will hand u a fur mask
& an electric eel   & U will b saved

U WILL BE SHAVED!!

〜〜 The Yumfactory 〜〜

JU-JU JEZZY *(a moping jellyfish)*: Fresh out of rehab, hey, Princess? Did they do you up right in the Gate of Heaven?

XXX: Fuck off. Anybody seen the Sea Witch? I gotta li'l problem I need her help with. Is she in her lair?

COCO LE SOB *(a randy dolphin)*: God help you if she is, Smutkins.

[XXX enters the Sea Witch's lair, a crepuscular sea cave deep beneath the rumbling Yumfactory.]

SEA WITCH *[muttering to herself as she pulls grey organs out of a plastic bag]*:

I perch on heaven
habitually
Pig-sized
nipples

Nerves weaving into a hood   Nacreous skin popping
into feathers   Plink Plink

XXX:
I lost my strap-on + I'm hot for The Smear

SEA WITCH *[not looking up]*:
Loose the fish tail   Grrl
& Get yrself   a real snatch

Go 2 the loading docks
@ the back of the Yumfactory

Ask for the Jizzler

The Jizzler!

[XXX enters a room that looks like a Steampunk inventor's cabinet. Odd charts & machine parts lay scattered about.]

JIZZLER *[singing]*: A hey and a ho! And a G and a ho! Tra la la la!

XXX: So, um, u can score me a real snatch?

JIZZLER: Score u a snatch? Yes, ha ha! That's good! Yes, I can score u! Like an old skool phonograph record! *[Holds up a longish steel needle.]* You'll play only pussy!

XXX: I mean, like, I'll be able to feel shit?

JIZZLER: I can't grow nerves 4 u. But I can unmermaid u, if that's what yr asking.

XXX: It's not.

JIZZLER: Hold on!

XXX: Mmph!

XXX:
I go squelch
in my welkin

& hook up to
the Jizzler   What convo is this

What horned combo
of no + yelp +

I sing the bright prong
& the day gets gluey

Off with my fish tail

My prosthetic legs are retrofitted

The plastic snatch   smooth like a chestnut
snapped on
+ umph holes drilled deep

The undersea forests drip pearly tar
& The Yumfactory quivers

XXX: That's it?

JIZZLER: Yep. 25 doubloons, please.

XXX: My legs hurt! I can barely freaking walk!

JIZZLER [*winks*]: O puh-leaze! What's a little pain for a little pussy? [*Goes back to singing.*] A hey and a ho! And a G and a ho! Tra la la la!

[*XXX heads out across the sea floor to her father's undersea pleasuredome.*]

XXX:
O my pornological gelding
The sea
is closing in on us

Where do I penetrate Where do I slide right in O my grieving animal

XXX:
The Smear is
a weather system made of meat

I can taste his bones from here
with my anal spines

[*Walking on prosthetic legs is clearly laborious & painful.*]

XXX [*looking down at her new body*]:
I look like what I am

a goggling white
meatpuppet

Human cheese

[*XXX wiggles & her plastic legs & snatch pop off. Her tail instantly reappears.*]

∿ The Sea King's Undersea Pleasuredome ∿

[*The King of the Sea is first seen from behind, unstrapping a red gimp ball from his mouth. When he turns, we see he is ripped & magnificently built. He has five nipples.*]

KING OF THE SEA:
The Daughters of Err

r totally   avantcore

They go craw-thumping with exobots

They get all swiggnotic
& whammo

but they don't touch mooncalves
like u do

XXX:
In the traumadome
u r the prince of whatnot
& I am nobody's daughter

In the slutosphere   O my hot father
u & I are no. 1

A Childhood Reminiscence

XXX:
Father   Lend me your megabone
& I'll lend u   my shotgun mouth

[Aside] With no cock in sight
how will I grow
my milkteeth into clitoral clouds

KING OF THE SEA [*looking out over his dominion*]:
Yr iced hips & choral work
r

the fatality of my animal   Marked off by delirious swelling
of the cloud-boned mercantile class

My stains hang lo   over the rioting submarine city

XXX:
Mmph.

KING OF THE SEA [*taking XXX's hand & leading her towards a new chamber*]:
Dotter   U r a toppled organism
Yr desire doesn't suit u

Come with me 2 fitter climes

I've arranged a sea-pasture of suitable animals 4 yr maxi yum

XXX [*entering the chamber & seeing the dazzling spread of creatures*]:
I'm reeling around in my blubs
My bones dripping out

If I'm not cockgobbling by half past a lunar rabbit
Let the pageant begin

[Intermission.]

XXX [*wiping assorted fluids off her cheeks & mouth & exiting the Pleasuredome*]:

My nerves are in their infancy again

O mellifluous nights of jelly munching
In a hale breeze

u can positively smell the deboning
of paradise   My sweet fucker

My demonology
drives me back to the killsite

where The Smear first said
Boo

I take a skull dump
& dream of pumping

my snog muscles into yr facehole
My skull bags collapsing

I'm totally sick
of the liquid realm

so I smoke the sauce pipe
& do some liquid bling

& go to see the Sea Witch

Bratface   I tell her
I'm vextipated
in my boo shank

I need some varmit to crank my jank

Some varmit   exactly like
The Smear

She nestles my tongue
in a box of salty cupcakes

chops off my tail
& sets it on ice

♥ ♥ ♥

SEA WITCH: As long as The Smear wants to tap yr shizz, you can keep your human form. He loses interest? You're iced. You forfeit your life.

XXX: Um, no freaking way!

SEA WITCH: No deal, no Smear!

XXX: Christ. Fine.

XXX:
On land I jibber-jabber
Eee eeeing like a dolphin
Toddling about on my bowling-pin legs

Look at me now
I'm a sexoid gooch snuffler

crawling straight out of my own private freakopolis

On land all the gill-babies like me
are sicko in the smack glands

Dump kitties
& ass clowns   turned blubberwocky

A nacreous stink
stealing into their kill buds

Is this some avant-turd jank off
The Smear's mother shouts

as I toddle up the castle lawn
on bowling-pin legs

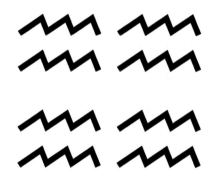

{The people on land.} {Look like large hunks of uncooked bacon} {suspended from walls} {in plastic medical bags.}

{At a meat brothel.} {You can sculpt the cocks} {any way you like.} {Cocks of solid grease.} {Of gristle.} {I prefer deer cartilage + bone struts + rabbit fur} {with chrome rims.}

{The meat puppets have} {moveable assholes.} {Moveable mouths.} {Paste-on-able hair of varying lengths.} {Clusters of 5 or 6 balls.} {Delicate jizz pipes exposed} {like wires.}

{Dip the puppet bodies in wax} {to make a thick casing.} {Dig into the wax skin} {& pull the meat stuffing out.} {I'm fingers deep} {in their ground chuck faces} {when I cum.}

LAND-DWELLER [*stepping into light*]:
Seems you made quite a spectacle of yourself over at the castle. It's not every day some piece of inhuman filth with prosthetic legs and a voicebox comes toddling up on land.

XXX [*quietly, with cartoon Xs for eyes*]:
Uh-oh.

LAND-DWELLER [*moving closer*]:
It's illegal for mermaids to even be on land. And a mermaid in a Meat Brothel? Shocking!

[*Police appear. XXX starts to back away.*]

LAND-DWELLER:
Crawl back into yr sewer, u slimoid cunt.

[*Police officers grab XXX, who struggles and kicks. She bites one hard in the cheek. They stick her with a tranquilizer.*]

XXX [*kicking + swooning*]:
Open up o slut sky & let me roach into yr cruel edicts

Gas me now
or
suck my
throbbing goats   U drillholes

∿∿ ∿∿ In Quarantine ∿∿ ∿∿

[*XXX is placed in a solitary cell in a RE-EDUCTION CAMP 4 THE SEXUALLY DEVIANT. Unknown to her, The Smear is also being held in the men's community cell.*]

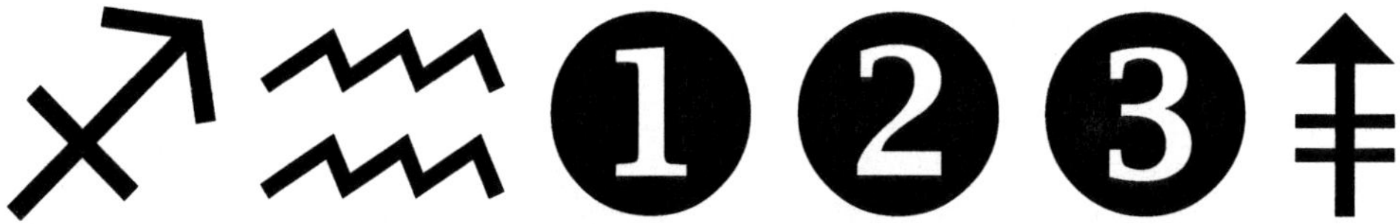

OCTOWARDEN [*over the loudspeaker*]:

YR SHELL BODIES WILL BE REMEDIATED INTO NORMS

THIS IS REPRODUCTIVE CAPITAL

THIS IS DESIRE PUT INTO THE SERVICE OF THE STATE

OCTOWARDEN [*scanning the cells, where most inmates are now sleeping*]: The Orphaned Nihilist Society runs a program to rehabilitate the worst of these offenders.

NEW OFFICER: What kind of program?

OCTOWARDEN: O you know, drug them, dress them in drag, make them do public performances, whore them out. The usual stuff.

NEW OFFICER: The Orphaned Nihilists? Aren't they a bunch of pirates and slave traders?

OCTOWARDEN [*pointing to The Smear*]: And they're coming for that one tomorrow.

NEW OFFICER: What's he in for?

OCTOWARDEN: His last "girlfriend" was a hermo.

NEW OFFICER: A homo?

OCTOWARDEN: No, a hermo. A hermaphrodite.

NEW OFFICER: For realz? Like she has two sets of junk?

OCTOWARDEN: Like her mutant shiz was so scrambled you couldn't tell what it was!

OCTOWARDEN [*approaching The Smear, who's lying awake, & gesturing toward XXX*]: So how d'you like that hot little slice of mermaidy cooch?

THE SMEAR: She can't speak. She's just a doll. But she can close her eyes. One blink for yes, two blinks for no, three blinks for paradise. She blinks twice as the soldiers drag her into the discolored bath water.

OCTOWARDEN: There's no freaking bath in this grothouse.

THE SMEAR: That this pool was made of cattle bones only makes the situation more special.

OCTOWARDEN [*knitting his brow*]: You tweaking, or what?

THE SMEAR: There is something curiously wrong with my mouthpiece. The porcelain has browned and the exoskelton has soured.

OCTOWARDEN: Probably because you're an Air-Breather, asshole?

THE SMEAR: There is a travesty about foreign bodies. They're counterfeits. We don't know how to wash them properly.

OCTOWARDEN: You freaks deserve to lie in your own filth.

THE SMEAR: A foreign body is always a nonproductive body. Non-reproductive. Always reproduced. Ghastly and flat.

OCTOWARDEN *[yawning & looking bored]*: So which garbage flotilla are you from?

THE SMEAR: We live inside The Meadow. That's not the true name of the hotel, but that's what I call it because of the lamb masks.

OCTOWARDEN: C'mon. You're shitting me. There are no more meadows. Not a shred of green left after the wars. Everything living gone rancid.

THE SMEAR: There's a rancid quality about Art that I have always thought made me susceptible to hospitalization.

OCTOWARDEN: Hello, freak? This is a rehab unit for the sexually deviant? Not a hospital?

THE SMEAR: I make a spasmatic pose for the penal colony. I wear a gas mask for the finale. The tourists are allowed to take my photographs if they first offer me some food.

OCTOWARDEN: No visitors! No snacks! Do you even freaking understand that you're under arrest?

THE SMEAR: In The Law, I wear a torn plastic bag on my face and my body looks like a girl's body drowned in a creek. I photograph well.

OCTOWARDDEN: Drowned girls, now you're talking! A little snuff porn always pumps my 'nads!

THE SMEAR: I chew gum, but it won't help my genitals.

OCTOWARDEN: Ok, whackjob. Whatevs. C'mon, you're really not popping wood for that mermaid hottie?

THE SMEAR: She must be an allegory. But it might be that I am not. Or she is not, and everything she touches is removed from the allegory. My penis for example is now meaningless.

OCTOWARDEN: O what, now you're a vrigin or something? That little bitch is a total hottie jizzsocket!

THE SMEAR: My virginity is redundant. My concussion is blatantly ornamental. We are ornamental. Like bodies piled into patterns on a screen.

OCTOWARDEN *[laughing]*: O I love to watch me a good bukkake scene!

THE SMEAR [closing his eyes as though in pain & turning away]: I'm a moralist for the zero mouth. Cockdead. I've guzzled way too much porn.

XXX [*straining to hear*]:
OMfuckingG

Cockdead

How can I make it   so that you will never have existed

With my good head
I wipe you clean

〰〰 The Crypto-Real 〰〰

JU-JU JEZZY (*a moping jellyfish*): What's wrong with her?

COCO LE SOB (*a randy dolphin*): She's been lying on the sea floor for days. Looks like she cut off her own tail. An amputee.

SNARLA (*an electric eel*): Yikes! She's got a nasty colony of flubworms in her swim bladder!

COCO LE SOB: Someone should harvest her organs. Good price on the black market.

JU-JU JEZZY: O right, turdbrain! Harvest organs from the King of the Sea's own daughter?

SNARLA: What's she watching on that crap-ass TV?

COCO LE SOB: Seal porn, u doof. All the young girls are into it.

XXX [*slurring*]:
My dream glands
           luxuriate   in posthumous suckholes

           Wetly I die
In castles of vermin spooge

SEA WITCH [*crossing the sea floor toward XXX & mumbling to herself*]:
My bunny's shot + sticky

Wadgobbly

I'm in a post-candy drill   w killer cells

Dirty balloons + rods   Altered pink shell fringe

        wobbles onto cremation grounds

SEA WITCH [*sees XXX & smiles crookedly*]:
O there you are. Get up.

XXX: I'm bleeding to death!

SEA WITCH: O for Christ's sake! Get up! What happened to you?

XXX: I got caught in a meat brothel and spent a week in reeducation camp. And The Smear doesn't like me. [*Cartoon X's for eyes*] Sob!

SEA WITCH: Bullocks!

XXX: I'm not cut out for this.

SEA WITCH: If you are cavorting in the fleshdrome
with the neo-animals
My pet
It's surely because   you have the chops

[*She spits on XXX & her tail instantly regrows.*]

SEA WITCH: Get the hell up.

XXX: You said I had to forfeit my life!

SEA WITCH: Never mind what I said. Kill The Smear, and you can keep your precious life. And your snatch.

XXX: Kill him? Um. No.

SEA WITCH: Your choice. Take this, in case you change your mind. [*Hands her a knife.*] He'll be on stage at the Yumfactory tomorrow night. In a show put on by the Orphaned Nihilist Society. It'll be. A gas.

XXX: The Orphaned Nihilist Society? Aren't they like an artists' collective or something?

SEA WITCH [*laughs*]: Exactly!

∿∿ The Royal Theater ∿∿

The Orphaned Nihilist Society Presents
* A GHOULISH OPERETTA *

[The Royal Theater is packed. Giant lipstick worms spew huge pearls that float out over the audience. Enormous golden scallops open & close. Scarlet steam vents open in the sea floor & phosphorescent moon jellies

drift out by the thousands. The King & Queen are in attendance with their royal retinue.]

STAGEHAND: Third act, bitche$$$! Let's bounce!

[*The curtain opens. The players sing sloppily & slur, their heads lolling. Corpses & crackling kabuki music & tinny voiceovers. Tied to the undersides of tiger sharks, the players wear heavy pancake make-up. The few who are still alive appear drugged. Their gender is all garbled. One player enters tied by the hair to a shark's tailfin, dangling badly & knocking over set pieces.*]

QUEEN [*clapping giddily & barking like a seal*]: Advances in theater! How exciting!

PLAYER 1:
She that diapers the dead: I defy thee. Eat my creaky ass plates.

THE SMEAR:
Art thou a beard?

PLAYER 1:
No, monster. Blow me.

THE SMEAR:
B not a beard. The cosmetic aisle is full of noises,
Sounds & crude bleats that delight & hurt, haha.
Yr bum about mine ears rejoices, etc.
Sometimes my thousand dangling instruments, etc. [*blearily grabs crotch*]
The clouds methought would open & show bitche$$
Ready to drop upon me, etc. When I waked,
I cried 2 cream again.

[*XXX darts onto stage, riding on a giant jellyfish. The switchblade glints in her hand. The audience thrills.*]

SEA WITCH [*leaping to her feet & spilling her popcorn*]: Kill the blaggard!

[Enter a chorus line of corpses, all bound together with heavy ship's rope. They are dragged back & forth across the stage while the kabuki music pops & crackles.]

XXX:
I'm wearing my body like a famine bird
like an occult door prize   gaping mid-riot

O incorruptible
I'm trashing the gates of your cumpacked republic

I'm getting janky in the killbuds
A firebrat
          in my gillysuit

QUEEN OF THE SEA [*shrieking at XXX*]: Shrimpface, this is televised!
You're on national TV!

XXX:
On national TV   I'm totes brillz
w yakkies
        in my fishbelly   & Blood thunder in the aerodrome
as I pop a bunny
tying yr arms back

THE SMEAR [*smiling*]:
You've done this before!

XXX:
Blabberpuss

Eat my serial displeasure
Eat it large & fast & hard

[*XXX moves to strike. The Smear blinks up at her sleepily.*]

[*XXX kisses The Smear. The audience roars.*]

[A giant explosion rocks the Yumfactory. Huge pieces of ceiling come down & the stage cracks in half. Insurgents have attacked the theater, slyly assisted by The Orphaned Nihilists. The King flees with his retinue, leaving the Royal Guard engaged in fin-to-fin combat.]

THE SMEAR [*looking intently at XXX*]: Mutiny. Cockhard. Queer. A newfangled disease.

[*The theater is in total chaos, everyone trying to escape. Rogue insurgents cut the ropes that bind all the players, most of whom sink to the sea floor. Tiger sharks begin to feed. The Smear, now alert & having narrowly escaped the Royal Guard, grabs XXX by the shoulders.*]

THE SMEAR: We'll do the brilliant cuckoo with your hands tied above your head. We'll do the angry cuckoo against the wall. We'll do the cracked cuckoo on glass. We'll do the leaky cuckoo. The sweet cuckoo.

XXX [*breathless*]: Say that again?

THE SMEAR: Meet me at my castle. Tomorrow at midnight.

XXX: Um, sure. [*The Smear flees*.] OMG!

BLUBBER SOCKET [*in low tones*]: Has anyone mentioned to her that boy's a porn freak and a sadist?

PURSED & PUCKERED: Of course, she knows. Why the fuck else.

KINDERWHORE: Those are just stoopid rumors. Cuz he's an orphan. And a former slave.

CINDERSKELLA: Hardly. He's like her own private Slice Ward. I heard he's even got a replica of The Gate of Heaven.

〰〰 The Isle of Noise 〰〰

[*Nearing midnight, XXX is waiting for The Smear at his castle of bone. She swims in an opening among the trash piles.*]

XXX:
How long will this stellectric meat knot take

In the suckshack

will his face finally debase me &
unbuckle
        My junk flinching pinkjoy   eggwhite noise spurt

Is the spectacle happening now
        in the calcified docking zone

Is it happening now

Is this a relationship
or just
a confused noise

[*In the near distance, the Smear climbs onto the garbage flotilla.*]

XXX:
My seal meat vibra-flounce +
flutter buttons

Ring-a-ling

The Gate of Heaven

[A series of lewd, erotic pics of XXX & The Smear skipping about in fishnets & engaging in coitus in piles of rotting sea creatures. They draw fake wounds all over each other's bodies with red markers. They are doing embarrassing things with baby squid.]

In frankentime   I wag my humanalia
in yr foaming mouth

In foamtime   I am a narcoleptic monstrette
falling asleep mid-spasm

This is the de-narration
of everything I've ever known

This is the evacuation of the memesphere
4 some hottie tottie cocklove
& a little cloud blindness   in parking lots

My lyric putty awake
in yr boss hands   In the goatsong rising out of yr cumbanks

This is my antifluke

This is crystallography at the level of yr face floating wide through
  my animal dysphoria

Sea Lore

XXX & The Smear get junked up in the swanlight. After some time, XXX spontaneously grows a snatch. The Smear's cock goes up & up & up.

Fleeing pirates, they join a grime art cell. A rogue art collective. Necrofantastic, illegal, lowbrow. A roving spectactacularium. They travel through riots and flaming cities, leading lives of ornament & crime. Cannibalizing themselves in2 art.

They sign high-rolling contracts as models for the House of Slop. They party down. They are hawt 4evah.

BOOTY CALL

Nearly all of The Smear's lines have been snatched/remixed from the poems of Johannes Göransson.

This book would not exist without the constant chatter, ambient noise & hard-core support of Danielle Pafunda, Jennifer Tamayo, Kate Durbin, Carina Finn, Laura Mullen, Becca Klaver, Feng Sun Chen, Alissa Nutting, Kate Zambreno, Kim Vodicka, Adam Atkinson, Andrew Shuta, Joyelle McSweeney, and Johannes Göransson.

And all the rest of you hooligans. Thank you for your crimes.

♥ ♥

Lara Glenum is the author *Maximum Gaga* and *The Hounds of No* (both from Action Books) and the forthcoming *All Hopped Up On Fleshy Dumdums* (Spork Press). With Arielle Greenberg, she is the co-editor of *Gurlesque: the new grrly, grotesque, burlesque poetics* (Saturnalia Books). She teaches in the MFA program at LSU.